To Elinor Finkelstein —
with appreciation for your support,
Marjorie Fleicher
Jan. 24, 1974

US: WOMEN

with an Introduction by Jean Valentine

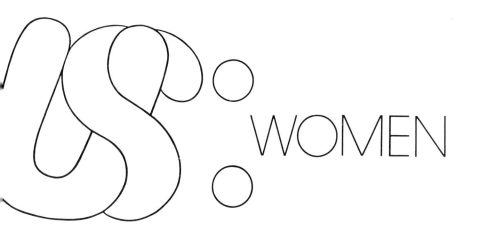

WOMEN

MARJORIE FLETCHER

Grateful acknowledgment is made to the following periodicals:
Arion's Dolphin, Boston Magazine, Hudson River Anthology, Let's Eat The Children, Rapport.

ALICE JAMES BOOKS
Cambridge, Massachusetts

For:

Joan, Patsy, Liz, Jody, Janet, Ala,
Cynthia, Jean, Connaught, Bobby,
Dorsey, Judi, Mollie, Ann, Marcy,
Beccah, Trina, Emily, Helen, Lisa,
my mother and Pam.

CONTENTS

INTRODUCTION

This is an odd, uncomfortable book, sometimes oddly moving, about a woman, and others. The woman in the book watches daytime TV, she reads Virginia Woolf, she fucks, she goes to parties; she has a child, she is single; she lives in a residential hotel, a commune, a suburb, cities. She is like a visitor from Mars, who reads *all* the literature and doesn't find her sex, her experience, her self, there. She decides to "write her own".

Notes, questions, jargon, graffiti: she uses cheap, everyday materials, whatever catchwords are at hand: orgasm, fantasy, the "bruising penis", "the whore,/ dangling nipples out of his reach",

> *the priest* [who] *decided to marry/ the twice married, once widowed mother who's 24./ That's what I wanted, wanted for them.....*
>
> *the man* [who] *looks at his watch: 12 o'clock: his tongue in my mouth/..... he laughs.* * *

> * * *& laughs. & laughs. & laughs. & laughs.*

It's a splintery job. The notes are abstractly graphic, innocent, corrosive, raw. They refuse to get up and dress and be poems. They're not friendly.

But neither is this voice easy, or familiar: not indulgently angry, fashionably monstrous. Not, either, petulant, that "fretful anxiety" that William James called "frivolous." At its best, original, flat, urgent, the voice stays with us:

You have not woken up. You lie on your back spread
naked on the double bed.
Sam in a corner plays with his trucks, eats
crumbs he picks from a tractor tread.
I answer the knock at the bedroom door: Sam's teacher, concerned.
I start to explain but her
mouth on your mouth, teeth in your skin .....

Gradually the persons in the book take on more particularity, grow more alive and familiar and strange. The woman's questions become (especially in the course of the long last section, the *Appendix*) the questions of human risks: the risk of nurturing, of friendship, of change; and the risk of witnessing — not being (necessarily) pleasing, or pleased — witnessing, telling. Keeping all the edge of that curious, green, Martian's eye view; an awkward, restless, honest presence, that won't sit down and talk, and won't go away.

— Jean Valentine

PREFACE: WOMEN ON SEX

ORGASM

If he's holding his body up

marking time with a $\frac{4}{4}$ thrust

he might raise my legs to his shoulders

and hurl   me

out

beyond Earth

beyond Mars

voids

exploding

Planet Y:

aliens celebrate The Fourth Of July.

FANTASY, THE DOMINANT POSITION

Aggressive, I roll   slowly   up, letting him know what he's in for.
I watch his face   and unmoving   astride him   watch him wait, him
wait. When he can't anymore, he presses his penis in   and the whore,
dangling nipples out of his reach, weaving from side to side, sees
images (obelisks* and colorslides) until: her husband is useless rags.

---

*   i.e., Bunker Hill or Washington's Monument.

MARIA ORTIZ

(For Michael Casey)

Today the priest
decided to marry*

the twice married, once widowed mother who's 24.
That's what I wanted, wanted for them. They deserve
both of them good. And the trouble they'll go through
his mother, goody church women won't understand, her son.
What a mess! But they both have it coming, both of them.

* Ms. Ortiz refers to events on "The Secret Storm", a daytime
television serial.

ADDENDA TO NEW YEAR'S EVE

A man looks at his watch: 12 o'clock: his tongue in my mouth.
When I resolve to do more for myself, he laughs.*

Hard, and huge as a fist his penis is bruising ..... *Bug off.*
Bug off. Are you deaf? He laughs.**

* His body is made like safety glass. It cracks when he laughs.
** & laughs. & laughs. & laughs. & laughs.

8

A SINGLE WOMAN

Too tired, but
she has said that for three days. Now she's afraid to resist.
She imagines:

she is dressed, standing next to the bed, watching him fuck the hollow
" ... life-size woman, built like Raquel."*

---

* "The Inflatable Woman"; *Wrestling World Magazine*: Spring 1973

INFIDELITY

Noon.

(You ought to be at the office.

Our son should be in school.)

You have not woken up.   You lie on your back spread

naked on the double bed.

Sam in a corner plays with his trucks, eats

crumbs he picks from a tractor tread.

I answer the knock at the bedroom door: Sam's teacher, concerned.

I start to explain but her

mouth on your mouth, teeth in your skin.   Tongues split your thighs.

POEM BY AN ANONYMOUS WOMAN

Like salmon they swim just under the surface, mechanics and suited men
bound by lines of the ink ruled cross-sections found in geology books.

BEGINNING JOURNALS (KAREN'S POEM)

We move on mudtide unmeasured through time

same season, same season, same wailing and sighs

voice among voice in the teeming mudpond.

(1)

Hear my voice
distinct
from others.

See form
with arms   with legs
a vagina.

See me
separate   whole   defined.

See

The independent form of a woman

Welling

Mud like concrete

Half-out

Coated .....

But: *you* take her part.* Pretend

* Or see the appendix.

17

you are that woman)

At last on solid ground, your energy spent, suffer the blanching heat.
Move no more than any wreck, but heave as sand sharks belly-caught.

Soon, and slow (like sundazed snakes) lesions grow, lesions break.
Blood in pattern dries: or caked, blood knives in your lengthening wounds.

See pines sway on the upper beach?
Think of a forest — unexplored, damp in shade and filtered sun —
Of stones that plunging miles in mist rush toward land you cannot see.

Now: toes over, your weight in your head, you are fighting the edge.
You are digging your heels, bruising the bark —
O, the pull, the incredible pain — forcing your face to the sun.

————————————————————

Karen sits on a rock, water-dark and smooth. She dabbles moss.
She dabbles moss. She is mouthing words to her own soundless song.

Song

Who stole the baby from its Mother's womb?
Life took the baby from its Mother's womb.
Time took the baby from its Mother's womb.
No-one steals a baby from its Mother's womb.

Who stole the baby from its Mother's womb?
Life took the baby from its Mother's womb.
Time took the baby from its Mother's womb.
No-one steals a baby from its Mother's womb.

Song

Karen

is defining Karen
is angry
is, screw you!

Karen
is angry, is grown-up, is
not you! is

Karen
defining Karen is
Karen.

maple oak cedar pine, linden elm yellow birch
poplar dogwood bayberry bush, juniper yew deadly nightshade
lichen moss indian pipe, mushroom puffball rabbit-turd
stream fern:

      a looming house, weathered, lights, someone home
door splintered, knocker and sign, THE COMMUNE WELCOME INN.

My name is Karen. I am twenty-four.
I need a bed, a place to write.
WELCOME INN, WELCOME INN

A 24 hour blare: light — on cots, on pallets on the floor,
on panties crusting menstrual blood, on poker games, on
petty theft, on fucking, on kids in bed with tonsillitis
The cat shits in the shower   Dinner is in three shifts
Venice In Season: Grand Central Station: Commune Welcome Inn.

(And everyone she has ever known is moving in next door.)

She has headaches everyday at four.

She imagines a brain tumor and doctor's date-of-death.

She imagines, with one year left, release and energy to name all names.

Her sister is pronounced insane. And when the family gather, she sees: reasons strike the air more solid than bodies, lies that feed again on childhome, a sudden growth, a bloom: her parents are demanding their own realities. Karen writes

LISIE, LEAVE MADNESS ALONE

I am, with you,
the world again.

I am the world
the only one
                I
spin without form
follow voice   echo of my own
searching Lisa, coming home.
But

light
without shadow of lie!
Lisie, I cannot.
Come out
Come out

24

(2)

Dear Virginia Woolf,

I have bought, but not yet begun, *A Writer's Diary,*
A Room Of One's Own: be whole.

Bare the force before the form. Show anger and despair
at home. Write, 'God, I hate Leonard today!' Tell me
why you had no children. Pile detail on detail. Be personal,
historical. Say Father. Mother. Name doubt. Name fear.
Expose.

The threads that control us. And, O, how they violate.

Sincerely,

(Karen Stone)

This book is not for publication.

September 2, 1972

*To record without order or discrimination: what a child I
have been. I will move in that direction.*

(The journals have begun.)

Sept. 3rd

*Someone has formed an amplified band. They are practicing
for 'The Big Break'. I can't read: I can't write: growing
boys need more sleep. I am fantasizing about: murder and,
moving out.*

next day

*Groans, yelps, somersaults — this is Commune Neverstop.
I ride the wave, my nose just out. I breathe. I rote-recite:
everything I know about myself.*

Sept. 9

*That wave, that sound, is in me now. The voices mingle so,
I can't identify my own. One — more than others — is
strong, compelling. Is it Mother twenty years ago? Is it
me?*

*I feel I am drowning
Or I have drowned.*

Sept. 10

(No entry)

——————————————————————

packing cartons.

marking each three times with her name, *screw you,*

she is leaving

Clothing, corner curled paperbacks straining the seams

(women, day-paled lights)

and the ball-point pens falling from her rucksack are unseen by

Karen walking not through green forest, but

women laughing

a Portuguese restaurant

barrels of rice and beans

a car with its horn stuck

a cop

a disabled car on the curb

children in twos or threes

a shop selling Indian silk

a retching drunk

Pot City

The Jazz Hut

Jullio's Liquor Mart

neon

Toilet

Telephone

Other Door,

Please

Dec. 2

*I have rented a room, with my oldest friend. She is
thinking about: children, husband, and how they keep
her from — Pam-doesn't-know-what. Other boarders:
artists, writers, academics. Monday nights we view,
or read, our current work.*

(Undated)

Form is my pivot. It is the least and the most important.

Dec. 13, '72

*Pam has bought marzipan. Windows in large department
stores, million dollar scenes: whole families from Medford
or Southie nose-press against the glass. Yesterday, in
Lincoln, even the snow was clean.*

Note: I am always depressed on the 26th.

32

The 2nd of January

roses root
outside,
push past the
door crack
into my
bedroom
and climb
one wall,
cover
one wall
with wood,
with thorns,
with flowers
that bloom
bitten
already
by some
vile thing;
branches strike
snow black,
pines move

January 8, 1973

My 25th

*1 hour 20 minutes, I dressed for lunch: I looked for
white hairs — found none: I wasn't convinced.*

*We walked. I needed a drink. But the bitch wouldn't
serve: I lacked proof of age. She served Pam (who is
younger): I sneaked sips.*

*This evening: the Monday meeting adjourns 11:30 then:
good grass, French food, cake, and* (word obliterated)
*celebrating my birthday, I am inviting everyone to the
Midnight Buffet.*

(We, accept the invitation.

Past an unchecked spread of candle wax,

Past the junior faculty defaming its new Dean,

Past poets scraping their plates or talking about Tate and Simic,

Past all these:

A woman is lying in bed.

She looks healthy, and dressed.

A translator sits in a chair by her side.

He is soaking his bread in *boeuf bourguignonne.*

He is singing a song we don't understand.

He tells us, she is dying.

APPENDIX

A.   NOTES FOR ALTERNATIVE ROLES

SCENES FROM A PROTOTYPE

1.

You hear the door banging. The door you just ran through.
The one with the wood frame, the bagging screens.
Someone pursued you.
Your daughter. She's 17, *and you think of yourself as 21.* She's out to
kill you.
(The house, weathered and rambling, is not on a farm.)

2.

A child appears.
She stands in the warm light, stirs dough with a wooden spoon.
Help. (Outside the screaming
voice of a woman, voice of your daughter who's 17, *Where have you gone to!
'll find you. I'll find you.)*

41

3.

The child says she cannot understand
can't understand but, tries
hides you behind forgotten boards that lean on the entrance wall

You hear the door

A WAR BABY DREAMS

She and her sons are viewing the Charles from a building on Clarendon Street. The day is amazingly clear and they lean, silence at the balcony edge.

From B.U. Bridge, jets, streak streak, jets, not fifty feet from the water.

One — *the fool* — loops; up, loops around; heading down, he does not recover. The woman, her children, watch "news-in-the-making", an Air Force jet crashing. And water thrown to such a height — beautiful, sculptural, female forms. Blast, tremor the very floor ..... is this what an earthquake is like? Her oldest boy floats up, feather drifting, out, beyond the balcony rail. He will fall. She cannot get to him. She cannot control her feet, cannot crawl. The building abutting spills roomsful of people from 5th or 6th or a 7th floor. Her second son slides, out of his mother's sight. More than a jet crash, this is

a bomb. She drops, arms protect head. Trying, — remember: what have you read about fallout, and how to avoid its effects.

IN THE RESIDENT HOTEL

(1)

In the lobby a woman, indented into the panelled oak, sells
newspapers, magazines — cigars, cigarettes.

A hair pin caught at the base of her neck bobs to a rhythm,
her own tuneless pleasantries. She is trying to make me feel
at home.

On the counter — magazines, small books. One by a woman whose
poems I admire. Covered red, about 8 x 10, it is bound with a
black, textured tape. Pushed through the tape

carpet tacks. They extend — dangerously past a coverless back.
Inside

not poems — prints, which unfold to poster size, drawn in
Beardsley-style, washed pastel pink and green. I ask.

I am told:

Ms. Turningheist lives twenty miles northwest, in the Jersey
hills you see from New York. She needs money and often brings
books. They take what she gives them. Sometimes it's poems —
sometimes it's not.

44

(2)

I walk across an empty lobby, past the over-stuffed chairs.
I enter a function hall. It has not been used in years. A
contractor sits on a plank he intends for minor repairs. I
sit next to him. He presses against me. He locks an arm
around my neck. He hangs a hand between my breasts. I am
not rude: I do not move. I wonder how I have encouraged
this. Someone begins hammering nails in the balcony across
the room. It is the contractor's helper, his son. He calls
to his father. He comes down to discuss the details of rail
construction.

The contractor is angry with his son: couldn't he see he was
spoiling things? couldn't he see I was almost laid? now I've
gone — I'm in the lobby again.

NOTES ON THE PLOT

The characters are:

> myself (I am 31)
>
> a boy who is either my brother or son
>
> the hero
>
> a man I don't know
>
> the hero's two henchmen

The setting is: our house, then the city.

First: we pretend we won't tell, we claim we are sincere.

The hero (I don't know his name, or age, but I have known him for years) commits crimes I block from my mind — murder is one, and the way that he does it.

It is clear that given a chance the man I don't know will inform. The hero stabs him (a gaping wound, the fall), covers the injured with paper the size of bed sheets but whiter, pushes his knife in at the edges stapling paper to floor, he pierces the flat, moving toward body, now blade prods at breathing, now — plunge. plunge.

I speak. I say it is okay with the boy and me. We are on his side. I say we need bread, I say we need milk, we will go out, go buy some.

We stroll. We stop at store windows, the boy and me. I, oh so casually, glance behind. The sun is warm. Vendors display iris and daffodil. I, oh so casually, am glancing behind me, walking, out of his territory, toward the police, their headquarters only a half block ahead of us. Now

the two henchmen, the hero's face, "Did you think you could get away?"

B. IF YOU WRITE YOUR OWN
— A DRAFT OF THE FORM

Childsong

help, murder, police
my father fell in the grease
I laughed so hard
I fell in the lard
help, murder, police

leaving home:

If she is a marionette

If some fist clenches white on her gathered string

— O

RÉSUMÉ

There was a little girl
who had a little curl

When she was good she was .....

Brearley graduate	'63
Radcliffe w/honors	'67
Summer in Europe	'68
Assistant to Editor (Random House)	'68 — '69
MFA Princeton (Daddy's school	

Heads you win
Tails I lose

She plasters lashes, a black backless dress on and screws all the salesmen who've heard from friends she's

Horrid	'73.

DOING TIME

The dog is   barking, circling

Children
       sliding down stair rails
           sliding down halls screaming
refuse to obey
              Someone is going
                  to let in a
                    monkey

      Musicians arrive.
      The clarinetist.
      The violist and his
      viola. The pianist and
      her assistant pushing a piano.
      The drummer, the
      bass drum and cymbals on wheels.
      The horn man. A
      cellist, an oboe, a
      violin, a violin, a violin

      while athletes push past.
      Athletes! wearing hats and helmets
      and face masks and padding, cleats
      red checked jackets, hip high boots;
      Athletes hauling reels and rods or
      pucks and sticks or bats and balls
      or rackets and
                Girls are
                    climbing
                the windows
         handing in

        homemade cookies dead flowers fish

        by the tankful   trunks   barrels

The delivery boys are coming:

They are bringing milk,
& coffee cake & whiskey
& laundry clean sheets
colliding at the doorway,
tripping over babies and drumsticks, slipping and .....
Let's eat

the children.

INVITATION

There is nothing worth stealing
here. We have all
we need. And sun and street
sounds. We have geraniums
in the window. But

have you seen how
the long-married couples
go into summer evenings
holding hands as if
they were closer by that?

We have music. And
grapes. You sketch
the world on paper
napkins. I love words.
We want nothing: but

have you seen how
they walk together,
how they talk and
smile, together
in the streets?

Listen: Today is
not yesterday or
its shadows. We are,
with a difference,
solid as concrete.

We can
risk the disappointing movies
or join some small parade
or envy lovers,
or walk
among the leggy girls
and the jawing law clerks
at the public fountain.

We can go now
into this city here.

JUNCTURE

The man I love has been seeing a woman I know.

I walk to a platform underground.

When the express comes, I do not board it.

I cross the tracks.

The man I love sits in an open subway car and the woman beside him.

They seem at ease.

She says they are engaged. I tell him *I don't believe it.*

She shows me her diamond engagement ring.

I climb to the street.

I enter a city. It is Paris. It is Spring

and the cobblestones gleaming.

ON THE EDGE OF SUCCESS

In a bus at the border of France women rummage their pocketbooks.

But she packed in a rush. She forgot her passport.

Officials board: they begin.

As women heft suitcases in the aisle, she slips

past uniformed men

(Does she get off the bus?

If she does, is she caught?

Could *you* cross a border?